Ugly Feet, OCD, and Other Intimations of Resistance

Aymon E. Langlois

ISBN: 9798878073059

Table of Contents

Acknowledgements *4*

Running Against the Wind:

Disabled Masculinity and the Vicious Cycle of Sport *12*

War Wounds:

Blindness, Resistance, and OCD in The Academy *41*

Cripping Heteronormativity:

Notes from a Relationship *75*

Acknowledgements

I am grateful for this opportunity to thank the people I love for the indelible marks they each have had on my life, work—my life's work—and my heart.

Thank you to Professor Linda Hall who taught me how to write acknowledgements and counseled me in the ethics of memoir. Thanks to Kate Crosby without whom I wouldn't have fallen in love with writing and Professor Barbara Black who is the reason I ended up writing at Skidmore College specifically. I am grateful for the friendship of Professors Cate Talley, Paul Benzon and Mason Stokes. Boundless gratitude to Professors Nicholas Junkerman and Susannah Mintz whose contributions are too numerous to adequately name, but who inducted me into disability studies and in so doing granted me an intellectual framework that's allowed me to love parts of myself society had me convinced were grotesque; for that I will be forever indebted to them...

Thanks to Ben Shahon for first believing in and giving this work a platform; "Running Against the Wind" was published first in *JAKE: The Anti-Literary Magazine*. Thank you to Cody Sexton at Anxiety Press for his endorsement and support of this work and for making this a joyous and liberatory entry into the realm of longer-form publishing.

To members of the disability community I worked with along the way: Bridget Coyer, Kimberly Pienkawa and Ellery Shea; Jillienne Glodowski, Carter Jones and Caroline Shea.

Thanks to my therapist Shinichi Daimyo who encountered much of that which is to come in rougher form and helped me work through it all.

At the recommendation of the aforementioned Ms. Linda Hall, I borrow and adapt from John Gregory Dunne in *Quintana and Friends* in offering the following: this work wouldn't have been contemplated, these pieces written, had it not been for one I shall not name, for our relationship ebbs and flows. But loving them, in all its imperfections, motivated me to integrate writing in my life—rather than have it consume me—and indeed life in my writing.

My love to the friends who feel like family: Lucie D'Entremont; Mary MacKeen and Tait Brencher; Spencer Evett, Charlie Stafford, Nora Weber, May Halm and Sarita Padukone; Morgan Sickels, Payton DeCrescente and Kylie Rowan; Genevieve Wasser and Vaughan Noble; Lea Leventhal, Henry Hamilton, Chloe Mickels, and Hunter Wasser. And to my family: the late Edythe Raymond; Jessica, Julia, Kate and Mark Webster; Edythe, Esther, Elizabeth and Yogi Howse; Andrew and Jeanne Rademaker;

Vivienne Langlois and Leslie Raymond. Security in your unconditional love equips me with the courage to write so vulnerably herein.

I dedicate this collection to my father, Stephen Langlois. Stacked against him the odds were. But he overcame mountains of childhood trauma to be the man I hope to become.

Ugly Feet, OCD, and Other
Intimations of Resistance:
A Narrative Suite On Disability
and Masculinity

Running Against the Wind:

Disabled Masculinity and the Vicious Cycle of Sport

I stand looking at myself in the mirror. I wear black Nike running tights. Nike isn't my brand but these are a favorite pair. I own three pairs and one can tell which are the favorites: the back pocket of the Nikes doesn't zip anymore; I've picked at the embossed logo on a pair of North Faces; the Sugois look new, they're taller in the back than they are in the front and are always slipping down which, on some level, makes me feel insecure about my waist size so I avoid them.

I'm shirtless. And I'm looking at myself. Not like Narcissus gazed at himself but rather doubtfully, critically.

Most defined are my pectorals and my abs taper pleasingly towards my navel. But other than that my chest isn't much to speak, or write of. And I dislike how my gut doesn't sit flat, or flat as I would like.

I suck in my stomach—it's a pressure that begins in my ass and shoots up my lower back, revealing the six slightly toned partitions of my abdomen that, since eighth grade, I've been manifesting with progressively more compulsive sit-ups.

When Liriope gave birth to Narcissus she asked Tiresias, the blind prophet if her son "would live to see a ripe old age" (*The Metamorphoses* 52). "'Yes,' [Tiresias] replied, 'so long as he never knows," that is sees "himself'" (*Metamorphoses* 109). If I'd never been taught to look at myself and assign value based on what I saw I'd be living a happier life. But when Leslie gave birth to me there weren't any blind elders to be found; there was no one to caution me against the shortcomings and harms of an ocularcentric and ocularly obsessed world.

As I write Word underlines "ocularcentric" and again: "That word, that concept doesn't exist," it tells me; "That's just the way it is," the societal subtext reads.

I've been looking at myself in the mirror above the sink. I walk back to my room.

Above the dresser hang five medals: three age division, a first and second place overall. Lest the nondisabled amongst you wish to be, as disability and literature scholar G. Thomas Couser writes in "Signifying Selves: Disability and Life Writing," "reassure[d]" by a discursive narrative of overcoming—to have your "fear of disability ... assuaged, at least temporarily, by a best-case scenario" — this isn't that type of narrative (this narrative doesn't document a "narrator manag[ing] to achieve something thought ... impossible for a person with a particular condition," id est the blind man with hypotonia learning to run); I've always been a fine runner, but ableism has rendered my relationship to running fraught (204).

I open the drawer at the bottom of the dresser and thumb through running shirts; it's early November, too cold to wear a singlet or short sleeve and there are many of those: two from RunBelfast's Bug Run 5Ks, I seldom wear either, one makes my nipples bleed, the other one's huge and makes me feel like a twig; another from their 2022 Kilted Canter 5K; and one from the Malta 10K I ran earlier this fall. There are three light shell layers, too cold to wear one of those. I pick out a heavier tech long sleeve, green, from the bottom of the stack, I unfold it and put it over my head, I slide in my left arm and then my right. Each sleeve has a thumbhole and after I put gloves on, I pop my left thumb through its thumbhole. I don't pop my right thumb through its because on my right wrist I wear my Forerunner and if I cover it with my sleeve I won't be able to check distance, pace, heart rate, total calories et cetera. I loop my OpenRuns over my ears.

The Skidmore College logo rests on my left breast, over my heart, like some fraud student-athlete. The Nike Swoosh rests on my right. Again Nike isn't my brand.

The neon yellow ASICS (GEL-CUMULUS 24s) that rest by my feet are. A runner of nearly 40 years, my father wears their GEL-KAYANOs. When I resolved to take up running some five years ago now and my mother took me to Marathon Sports—not my father, I think he resented at first that I'd taken up his torch but as he's started running again (he broke his ribs in 2012 and subsequently took eight years off from the sport) we've begun to bond over it— I was happy to be placed in a pair of ASICS like I was carrying on some sort of father-son legacy.

The nape of the neck seam on one of my favorite ASICS racing singlets reads "Sound Mind, Sound Body." This seems backward and concurrently makes sense to me. Some days, running mollifies my anxiety. And other days, it makes me feel more secure in my virility and the solidity of my body, the miles and calories burned do; running takes the edge off my body dysmorphia. Regardless a "sound" body precedes quietness of mind. "Sound Mind, Sound Body" seems to be operating on an exteriorizing rationale (i.e. minds exist within bodies); indeed ASICS—I find looking all this up—is an acronym for the Latin *Anima Sana in Corpore Sano* or "a sound mind *in* a sound body." What it means to have a "sound" body—what it takes to convince myself of bodily "soundness"—fluctuates, often interpreted through the fluctuating state of my mind; it's a daily negotiation. But running can take me there, to that quiet place.

My feet look like such shit that I, a blind person, can tell standing up: my second toes are runner's toes (i.e. the toenails are raised slightly off their beds and by dried blood their undersides have been blackened). I'm too embarrassed to take my socks off anymore because, while normative masculinity generally exalts the exhibition of material intimations of the endurance of pain, an ableist society has taught me and I've internalized that my ugly isn't desirable ugly; I've learned to self-stigmatize and self-police.

I slip on socks before loosening the laces of my shoes and sliding my feet into them, I tie my laces.

In director Leif Tilden's *1 Mile to You*—based on Jeremy Jackson's novel *Life at These Speeds*—Coach K. admonishes Kevin Schuler: "You have to take care of your feet, you have to take care of yourself." When Kevin tells K. about his 100-mile weekly base K. exclaims: "I thought you were joking. Why?" But like Kevin runs chasing the voice of his dead partner Ellie I pound my feet for between 45 and 50 miles per week to quiet the howl of a ruminative ableist cacophony in my head. Maybe

I'm "nuts" as Henny tells Kevin he is, though I wouldn't use that word...I think that's the point—ableist society will do that to you.

Taking care of my feet isn't always the same as taking care of myself. My ugly embodies resistance and I have to stop hiding that away.

Outside the apartment, I get my watch set and tap my headphones—Ben Rector's aptly titled "Drive" booms to life with its toms driving it forward. And I'm off.

The night's dark and chilly, the breeze doesn't help.

Out of the apartments, onto Perimeter Road where immediately I am met with a hill—stride shorter, let your arms do the work.

I run past the sports center. I was there earlier for cross weight training. I always feel like a self-conscious twig in weight rooms, these theaters of normative masculinity, surrounded by all the massive men. I check my watch: 0.50 miles; 6:58/mile pace; 140 bpm; 35 calories burned, doesn't help me feel better yet.

As I run up toward Zankel, the wind roars. I can just make out Lizzy McAlpine's "all my ghosts" under the howl of the wind… "All my ghosts are with me … they know all of my habits," Lizzy sings…

When I am born my eyes don't look quite right… After a visit to the pediatrician, my parents are referred to the Ophthalmology Department at Boston Children's Hospital… There I am seen by Dr. Anne Galton.

I don't remember her, obviously, but looked her up once or twice: her head looks like a Lego with a snow-white hairpiece that's snapped easily on; her cheeks are freckled, apples withered that frame her nose and mouth.

One of my searches turns back a "Caregiver Profile" posted by Boston Children's to YouTube. Disdainfully, I watch her head bobble as she says: "When I was in medical school, you had to select rotations; I thought, 'Meh, ophthalmology, let's see what that's like.'" She immediately strikes me as condescending.

Galton is both accomplished and representative of the field: she graduated from Radcliffe College in 1962, Tufts University School of Medicine in 1966, and completed residency with Yale University; she's a professor of ophthalmology at Harvard Medical

School and director of the Pediatric Medical Retinal Service at Boston Children's Hospital.

She tells my parents at one of their appointments — after Children's decided that I'm not completely blind — "He'll never play sports." This is what a Tufts-Radcliffe/Harvard-Yale pedigree gets you. Indeed this is the medical institution.

As a scholar of language my interest is twofold. First there's no invocation of ability: she didn't tell my parents "He'll never *be able to* play sports," just simply "He'll never play sports." Second I'm vexed by the absolute universality of "sports." I could understand, if not accept, how—if I'd been completely blind—ignorance, of innovations like beep baseball, could have led her to say, "He'll never play any of the big four sports." But neither was I completely blind nor did she limit her claim to specific sports. What about a sport like rowing, hell powerlifting, requires sight? What about the Paralympics? For her and society, my impairment and sport seemed mutually exclusive, contrary to one another; sociologist Tom Gerschick explains in his "Toward a Theory of Disability and Gender": "age of onset …

influence[s] the degree to which [a person] is taught and subjected to gendered expectations" (1265). In other words, her ableism makes good theoretical sense; congenitally impaired men are seldom regarded as real men—hence they are never expected to live up to athletic masculine ideals. And in time I internalized this notion that I'd never be athletic.

Again I check my watch stats: 4.3 miles run; on pace with 6:52/mile; 155 bpm; 325 calories burned. Nearly halfway.

The wind gusts—I turn my cheek to it to block it. From my headphones

Elton John and Bernie Taupin's words wash over me… "Touch down brings me 'round again to find I'm not the man they think I am at home — oh no, no, no — I'm a rocket man"…

I'm 10 and trying to claim what is rightfully mine: an athletic, masculine identity. It's yard time for fourth grade at Joshua Eaton Elementary School in Reading, Massachusetts. I stand on the line of scrimmage where Tom's told me he's going to hand off the ball to me — because nobody would've been expecting it in retrospect. The patch of ground I stand on used to be grassy but has—by stampedes of rowdy boys playing touch football, that seldom remains touch—been so trampled over that now dirt's all it is. Their compulsive need to perform normative masculinity has disturbed the natural order of things.

Tom barks "Green 19, set hut!" and we're off; Tom hands the ball to me and I run, the other boys chase after me. Tom calls them off, he says, "Let him go." The subtext roars loud in my ears: "He can't hang with us."

Indeed Bongani Mapumulo, Poul Rohleder, and Leslie Swartz warn in "Physical Disability and Masculinity:

Hegemony and Exclusion": "One of the challenges faced by anyone who does not … fulfill dominant social roles is that others may patronise them — they may make allowances for them out of … condescension" (97).

I think of *ulwaluko* — unanesthetized circumcision, the Xhosa coming-of-age ritual for men. As the foreskin is being cut boys cry "Ndiyindoda!": this means "I am a man" in Xhosa; hence this process marks the transition of boy to man. But the *ulwaluko* process is exclusive — it takes place in the forests outside Xhosa villages; "[g]iven the physical location … and …

privations," Mapumulo, Rohleder, and Swartz write, "not all men with physical disabilities can take part in the process": lack of participation in this transition ritual denies disabled men their manhood—those who don't or can't participate remain labeled as "inkwenkwe" or "boy"—and "may lead to … psychosis" (96). For me and others I'm sure, schoolyard football was an analogous rite. This analogy may seem culturally belittling, ignorant and out of touch prima facie until one reflects on the absurd masculine and cultural capital we in America allot football. Boys may become anxious—in the absence of ritual markers of the transition from boyhood to manhood—to assert their masculinity and turn to sports, feats of strength and the endurance of pain like football. But these crude markers are exclusionary and able-bodied by essence. My inability—on account of my hypotonia and visual impairment—to meet some arbitrary standard denied me my masculine identity. Over time as I began to notice other bodies and realize that mine was being noticed too, this became increasingly distressing and eventually led to anxiety, body dysmorphia, and obsessive compulsive disorder. Sit-ups became running became working out at the gym, became bodily hyperfixation, became calorie-counting and purging with borderline exercise bulimia…

Scaggs' "Lido Shuffle" plays… "One more job oughta get it, one last shot 'fore we quit it — one for the road," Boz sings…

8.7 miles in, I am headed into my final lap of campus. My long runs are seven currently. I'm quite literally running in circles. I started running to allay anxiety, often bound up with body dysmorphia. The problem is that I've begun to conflate the euphoria of runner's high with relief that I've burned away my imperfections; instead of the endorphins and endocannabinoids, I attribute the decrease in my anxiety to miles run, calories burned. Thus I equate positive body image, admittedly strong and normatively masculine, to athleticism. This capitulates to and exacerbates a vicious cycle that was initiated some years ago in doctors' offices, on touch football fields; I say to myself "If I just get out for today's run I can finally be regarded as a man." It does afford me relief though… So I ask: am I quieting or enabling the ruminative ableist cacophony in my head?

As I run down the hill, toward the apartment, my feet slap against the ground. A physical therapist saw me for my hypotonia when I was in elementary school. I remember her chiding "Quiet feet!" I don't remember why loud feet were bad, just that—like hypotonia—they were and were something to be embarrassed of. When I run now I associate the shame of loud feet with the pounding and ugliness of mine—and try to quiet them down. But tonight, I'm not hiding, I'm not ashamed—I'm taking up space: I let my loud ugly feet sound into the night.

As I come to the end of this essay ostensibly about running and my fraught relationship with it, I realize I've done a relative dearth of writing about actually running; form might evince what I've been attempting to find through the process: my relationship to running isn't fraught, it's my relationship to everything running-adjacent that running helps me work through—running's the solace...

I traipse up to the mirror above the sink where I peel off my shirt and stand looking at myself. Still doubtful, still critical; still don't think my chest is much to speak of.

I suck in my stomach—it feels even less satisfying than when I went out:

when you run you get soft and at least what little I had before was solid. With sweat my sternum glistens.

But for today a run's taken the edge off; it's taken me there to that quiet place.

I haven't shut off my headphones yet, a song that I don't recognize has come on. A twangy voice I think must be Thomas Rhett sings: "If I'm honest, I am plagued by the fear that I am not enough, yeah, so I work hard to measure up: I've run a million miles; climbed a mountain high; felt the same when I was done… Is it the things you've done, the places that you've been, or is it making peace with who you are and where you stand? Oh

I'm trying to find what makes a man..."

War Wounds:

Blindness, Resistance, and OCD in The Academy

Disabled people are denied specific desired identities, like athleticism, sexuality, and intellect, by an ableist society to whom these identities seem inconsistent with disability: physically impaired people — unable to participate in culturally dictated exhibitions of strength and endurance — are denied their rightful athleticism; believed to be perpetual children counter to the spheres of adult pleasure, disabled people are labeled as "asexual" — denying allosexual disabled people their sexual identities; and, as a blind person, I've been denied my intellectual identity.

It's spring 2013: having either read or seen Suzanne Collins' *Hunger Games*, teens everywhere have pledged solemn allegiance to "Team Gale" or "Team Peeta"; Carly Rae Jepsen's on the radio; and I turn thirteen in August.

We travel with our homerooms in middle school. We are in science class with Ms. Duckshrub learning about precipitates; I'm working with a girl I have a crush on, named Rose, on an activity the objective of which is to identify the precipitates in a test tube of fluorescent blue liquid. Rose is brilliant. Like I, she's one of the few students who actually cares about this stuff. Next to us two a paraeducator, Ms. Maria, is taking pictures for consultation as I write my lab report. Rose delicately dangles the test tube as I peer in. Ms. Maria memorializes a moment.

At home, I look at the photo; I look at myself looking. I subject myself to my own stare and cry: there is something of Emily J. Harding Andrews' cartoons about me (Harding Andrews was a suffragette artist who caricatured and exploited intellectual disability in her pro-suffrage poster "Convicts, Lunatics, and Women! Have No Vote for Parliament"; the ridiculousness of the exclusion of women from the vote is brought out by the juxtaposition of woman with groups "sensibly" excluded from the franchise: the woman—in academic regalia—represents all that is enlightened, the "lunatic"—with back hunched and tongue out—patently doesn't). My head slouches toward the tube to afford my impaired eyes proximity, my mouth hangs open, flaccidly agape. A caricature, I'm even dumber than dumb and then there's Rose with her lustrous penetrating eyes. I rush upstairs to show the picture to my mother in bed. "I look retarded," I choke out.

I think it is interesting that I understood my need for spatial proximity as intellectual disability. I had imbibed unconsciously what is termed the seeing-knowing synonymy or metaphor, which David Bolt, author of *The Metanarrative of Blindness,* explains as "the idea that not seeing is synonymous with not knowing" (18). Metaphors of seeing and blindness are often employed as unchallenged everyday flippancies for knowledge and understanding or lack thereof: "see as"; "see how"; "see through"; "in one's view"; "view as"; "You see what I mean"; "How can you be so blind?" Sight, the only sense, as philosopher Jonathan Rée understands it, that can give us information without bodily contact, is privileged; Rée writes: sight is "more masculine than the contact senses. [It is] epistemologically … more respectable" (34). Blindness is correlated with ignorance also in cultural production. For example, in dramatist Brian Friel's *Molly Sweeney*, ophthalmologist Mr. Rice says of titular Molly: she "lived in a blind world" (38). Sweeney recalls that Rice asked her, "How do you think your world compares with the world the rest of us know" (Friel 36). Molly "live[s]" in her world, the others "know" theirs (Friel 38, 36). The more canonical John Milton writes of Samson: he was "blind of sight," "thought extinguish't quite" (*Samson Agonistes* line 1687, 1688). And in *Paradise Lost,* the poet laments that "thy sovereign vital Lamp [...] Revisit'st not these eyes" and that "the Book of knowledge fair, / Presented with a Universal blank" (Book III lines 22-23, 47-48). Though, perhaps most relevant to the context of this essay is sociology professor Rod Michalko's "'I've Got a Blind Prof': The Place of Blindness in the

Academy." Michalko writes: "The students in front of us have had … several years of *seeing the point*, of *not being blind to the facts*, of *looking at things objectively*, and of *trying to see what the teacher is getting at*. They have had many years of educational practice of seeing that seeing is enlightenment and blindness is ignorance" (76, emphasis added). The seeing-knowing synonymy is, in this way, a form of stigma, and as scholar Heather Love argues of stigma, "Once a person is stigmatized, other qualities tend to be interpreted through the lens of this trait" (175). "Observing me compensate for a visual deficit in this grotesque way," my thought process went, "people will assume another deficit exists beneath the surface." And indeed, this was around when prejudice began to reverberate in school hallways: "He's the blind one"; "special one"; "slow one"…

I wish I could say this bias was about loss of control of my narrative, rather than perceived undesirability of intellectual disability. Frankly, I wish I could say this bias was—that it was and was no more, that it had dissipated in my years academically studying disability.

But to say either of those things would be to deceive, designedly albeit subconsciously, both reader and myself: this bias is, it hasn't dissipated. Unconsciously I'm still ill at ease at the prospect of intellectual disability; my uneasiness issues from the state of affairs that intellectual disability represents what I wouldn't want to be, not because it is objectively negative but because it's antithetical to the resistance I have mounted to the ableist construction of my blindness. My discomfort with this form of human vulnerability — cognitive impairment, which frequently entails dependence — evinces my indoctrination in and complicity with the normatively masculine criterion of independence and my reluctance to disrupt that normalcy any more than blindness already does.

Again if I'd been cautioned against paying heed to others' perceptions of me... Instead, society foisted defensiveness upon me, a feeling that I need to substantiate my intellect.

In college—saddled with hometown acquaintance and prejudice no longer, able to begin again, to not be the sightless moron anymore—I was determined to normalize myself—disavow blindness as an identity and prove my intellect—deny this new community the opportunity to again preinscribe my narrative similar to the last.

As I stood on the proverbial threshold between high school and college, with regard to my visual impairment I opted to employ person-first language—and the choice came from a place of succumbing to ableism: I didn't want to be "the blind one" anymore—to be "special" or "slow."

With the corpus of disability studies at my disposal, "people with disabilities"—people-first language with respect to disability (as contrasted with impairment)—doesn't make sense:

disability, within the schema of a medical/social dichotomy between itself (i.e. what elsewhere I have called society's "myriad barriers to inclusivity") and impairment (i.e. bodymind limitations), doesn't inhere in a person. Ableist society foists disability — social exclusion — on impaired people. I prefer "disabled person" as contrasted with "person with a disability": while the noun implies inborn untampered-with reality, the participial adjective suggests the interference of external actors. Many activists argue the opposite way, that the adjective suggests inherence and "with" implies attachedness (I'm not convinced by this argument). PFL, in this context, also takes for granted that people yearn to relegate disability to second-rate status—that nobody really wants to identify as disabled, what it understands to be an objectively undesirable experience. But disability is a prideful and shared identity, like race, gender and sexuality, religious affiliation, etc. etc.

Still the question of person-first language with regard to impairment— the question I thought I'd answered once and for all, four years ago—remains vexed.

The choice to identify as a "person with a visual impairment" would no longer come from a place of appeasing ableist society; I'm not ashamed. Still my visual impairment does inhere in me, and, as much as I want to invoke the counterdiscursive concept of cripistemology, to assert without qualification that blindness is another way of being in and knowing the world, being unable to access visual material on a day-to-day basis is difficult; of course that's because we exist in a profoundly inaccessibly designed world but even so...

Impairment inheres in people, and sometimes, as disabled feminist Liz Crow writes in "Including All of Our Lives: Renewing the Social Model of Disability," this "[i]mpairment *in itself* can be a negative, painful experience" (219). Should painful identities necessarily be relegated — pushed aside? I don't think so. My difficulty doesn't countervail my pride. Blindness is no less a part of my identity than collective disability; it shouldn't be any more displaced than it's counterpart. This is to say nothing of the fact that society's estimation of blindness is informed by metanarratives and blind experience constructed by inaccessible infrastructure. This patently isn't how I thought when I first arrived at college — "person with a visual impairment" it was. "Blind person" it now is.

As a student of English, my intellectual defensiveness manifested in composition perfectionism (I browsed through the thesaurus for better words often etc.). Though, with comments on my work from professors like "you stopped and excavated expertly down through the layers of meaning here ... The vocabulary you wield remains one of my favorite aspects of your style," perfectionism began to transform, in time, into OCD—arbitrary, debilitating rules or, more accurately, imperious idiosyncratic impulses about writing. My vocabulary was a favorite aspect of my style; skimming through the thesaurus for better words became cross-referencing thesaurus and dictionary laboriously for the best word on almost every word I write.

The wording that comes to my mind immediately is "cross-referencing thesaurus and dictionary meticulously." Eyes squinting, I look up "meticulously" on my phone. Synonyms include: *accurately;   anxiously;   attentively;*

assiduously; carefully; closely; completely; comprehensively; conscientiously; correctly; deliberately; delicately; discreetly; earnestly; efficiently; exactly; exhaustively; extremely; faithfully; firmly; fully; gingerly; hard; highly; intensely; intensively; intently; intimately; jointly; laboriously; nearly; painstakingly; precisely; prudently; rigorously; scrupulously; sharply; strictly; thoroughly; thoughtfully; very; warily; and *wholly.* Too objective are *accurately, closely, completely, comprehensively, correctly, exactly, fully,* and *wholly.* I flag *anxiously* as a potentiality. Too positive are *attentively, carefully, intently, precisely, scrupulously,* and *thoroughly.* I flag *assiduously* too. Plain wrong are *conscientiously, deliberately, delicately, discreetly, earnestly, efficiently* (ha!), *extremely, faithfully, firmly, gingerly, hard, highly, intensely, intimately, jointly, nearly, prudently, sharply, strictly, very,* and *warily.* I don't like *intensively.* I flag *exhaustively, laboriously, painstakingly* and *rigorously. Anxiously* doesn't get at the context. *Assiduously* and *meticulously* elide the impact of the context. *Rigorous* is going to be quoted. To the dictionary. *Exhaustively* means "in a way that includes all possibilities." *Laboriously* means "in a way that takes considerable time and effort." *Painstakingly* means "with diligent care and effort." *Laboriously* it is.

My close reading work was "dazzling"; I started stopping every few words, interrogating their order much more closely...this carried over into my writing.

"This carried over into my writing" or, "into my writing this carried over"? "This" exists in the interstitial space between close reading and my writing in the first, it is literally being carried over. In the second, "this" already exists within the realm of my own writing. I think about the meaning and the context and opt for the first accordingly.

That first-year spring, after an OCD-fueled round of revisions, the praised paper was awarded the English Department's Distinguished Writing Award for the Essay. I tell myself the tendencies are what it took/what it takes to convince others of my intellect; the societally induced determination to continue resisting the blindness-unknowing equivalence only exacerbates them.

A year later, in April 2021, my paper "Covert Aestheticism: Disability and 'Narrative Prosthesis' in Stevenson's *The Strange Case of Dr Jekyll and Mr Hyde*" was awarded Skidmore College's all-college award presented to excellent examples of prose. The committee commended my "word choice"— describing it as "rigorous and precise"; this reinscribed beliefs that intellectual recognition is contingent on compulsively rigorous choice-making, the same dynamic with my "attuned close reading." They also lauded my "energetic syntax": my obsession with word order became my obsession with punctuation; again, I started stopping between clauses and asking myself "What punctuation links them together logically? Comma? Dash? Colon? Semicolon? Period? Ellipsis? Question or exclamation mark? Are parentheses indicated? Do they artistically need to be connected by punctuation...?"

My obsession with word order became my obsession with punctuation. Stop. *Again, I started stopping between clauses and asking myself...* Immediately, I rule out both question and exclamation mark and the utilisation of parentheses. *My obsession with word order became my obsession with punctuation,* comma, *again, I started stopping between clauses and asking myself...;* of the first clause a comma feels dismissive. *My obsession with word order became my obsession with punctuation,* dash, *again, I started stopping between clauses and asking myself...;* the clauses feel too connected by a dash. "Halfway" I tell my tired self. *My obsession with word order became my obsession with punctuation, period, again, I started stopping between clauses and asking myself…";* now the clauses feel too disconnected. *My obsession with word order became my obsession with punctuation,* ellipsis, *again, I started stopping between clauses and asking myself…;* an ellipsis feels too hesitant. I think ambivalently, "Only two more"; I'm beginning to fear I'm going to have to loop back around and start over. "Do they artistically need to be connected by punctuation…?" I ask myself. Can I trust the answer "No" that comes to mind or is it influenced by exhaustion...? *My obsession with word order became my obsession with punctuation,* colon, *again, I started stopping between clauses and asking myself...;* too connected again. *My obsession with word order became my obsession with punctuation,* semicolon, *again, I started stopping between clauses and asking myself...;* semicolon it is.

After another painstaking round of revisions, "Covert Aestheticism" was published in *Wordgathering*; and so the feedback loop persisted.

What does it mean for a man to transgress norms of rationality? What does it mean for a man to be out of control? What does it mean in academia?

In March 2022, I attended and presented on what I called a more social social model of disability at the Northeast Modern Language Association's Fifty-Third Annual Convention in Baltimore, Maryland. After my presentation, an older scholar, possibly tenured, came up to me and we got to talking about disability and access in academia. We talked about text-to-speech software, that as a blind person, I am familiar with but until recently was resistant to, and how not having your eyes on the page in the context of literary studies is immensely stigmatized; this censure and my own resistance is due to the way that sight is understood to be commensurate with mastery. And yet even in this space of rare understanding and joyous identification, I was wary of the reaction and refrained for reason of stigmatization from disclosing that I began using text-to-speech software in order to avoid triggering my OCD.

For two years now, I've been afraid of reactions and stigma. Hiding my OCD is difficult, and draining; writing takes considerable time and there isn't much I can...or want to do about it (after graduation my mother wants me to see a cognitive behavioral therapist; I'm not sure I want that though, treatment and "cure"). As at other institutions of higher education, Skidmore College's Office of Student Access Services doesn't approve student accommodation requests for extended time on writing assignments, like papers and essays (this results from the ableist imperative for speed in the academy — the efficient production of intellectual output). This leaves me and other disabled students in need of extended time with the burden of approaching professors with extension requests (as a result of the academic and general stigma against OCD, disclosure is often couched and euphemistic); thus the fear. This fear comes from two places. I am often in this configuration at the mercy of professors who don't understand and when extension requests become habitual — and for me they can't not — become frustrated and unreceptive. In these ways, academia is simultaneously a disabling institution and an institution inhospitable to disability.

My embeddedness in static masculine norms of independence exacerbates discomfort and the experience of hostility. I shrink for reason of being marked as dependent and unmanly from requesting OCD-necessitated extensions. This fear of being branded as dependent evinces itself still more in classes in which materials haven't been adapted for my low-vision: sooner will I risk being reprimanded for using my phone without authorization to take enlargeable pictures of inaccessible material so as to be regarded by my peers as self-sufficient, than request that those materials be made accessible and so be regarded by my peers as unmanly. The irony is that in these interactions, holding back renders me less assertive and thus less normatively masculine. Also, reluctance compromises me as a disability self-advocate; masculinity counterintuitively impinges on the experience of disability in this way. We'd normally think of disability as impinging on masculinity.

I yearn to proudly bear my OCD like a war wound, an unapologetic intimation of the resistance I have mounted, sustained on the battlegrounds of ableist society in combat against its construction of my blindness; after all, considered neurodivergence in many communities, OCD is "just another" form of cognition, just another way of

interacting with the world, my reading
and writing. I don't anticipate this being
possible in the academy, that fray of
tenure clocks and prolificacy, any time
soon; so to borrow and adapt the words
of queer activist Harvey Milk: *Out of the
academy and into the streets!* Out into the
world of service and activism. Into the
streets where I will continue to write, on
my own nonnormative terms now. Into
the streets of solidarity: into the streets of
mutuality where I don't need to explain
myself and my pride—I'm simply
understood; into the streets of
interdependence and assertiveness
where I can lean on my disabled brethren

and they can lean on me. Into the streets. Into the fight. For our rights. For our lives. For our pride. Into those streets.

Cripping Heteronormativity:

Notes from a Relationship

A favorite musician of mine Hunter Hayes said once of his song "My Song Too," "This is about [a break-up] and knowing that at the end of the day you can't be mad at them … At the end of the day they made me better for the time that we spent together; so this is a song of gratitude and appreciation as hard as that is to admit sometimes." In a remarkably similar way—maybe it's because I started conceiving of versions of this essay when we were together—I'd like to say this is a sorrow-induced plea composed in the hopes of getting back together. But hard though it may be to admit, this essay too is an expression of my appreciation. You told me in those first weeks together that no English words conveyed your happiness, that the French *l'allégresse* was nearest. And indeed, I repeatedly said that words were incommensurate, that they failed miserably at expressing my joy in being with you. But I'll take you at your word that *l'allégresse* does the joy we shared justice. *L'allégresse d'être avec toi* made me realise there's greater elation in this life — what Pater called "the given time" — than intellectual recognition (12). It inspired me to not only incorporate but prioritise that kind of joy in my life; indeed this collection of essays wouldn't be if it weren't for the joy of being with you. Our time together afforded me understanding of the love I bring to and need in relationships.

Walking in circles that last night you said to me, "I really wanted to love you how you needed," that you didn't feel you could. I reckon it's also true that if you weren't loving me how I needed, then I wasn't loving you how you needed either. That's hard to know and harder to forgive myself for.

It's 2:00 A.M. on a Saturday night and I'm sitting at my desk. The fluorescence of the builder-grade tube affixed to my desk wisps through the darkness of my room; I haven't turned the string lights on since you left — they remind me of you and nights together. From my tackboard, a photograph of us and two friends stares at me. I've taken down the other ones, tucked them away in my closet: throwing us away doesn't feel right (What have you done with remembrances of me? That necklace?). I'm reading transgender sociologist R. W. Connell's authoritative study of masculinities — an impressive tome. The storm of fatigue, low light and low vision makes it tough—even painful—to read. But I'm searching for answers so I press on… Hegemonic masculinity—the societally dominant masculinity—is necessarily heteronormative. That is, it conforms to heteronormative gender attributes, including stability—evidenced in the primitive but not yet obsolete role of male breadwinner—and rationality in men. Patriarchal ideology would have us believe that relationships exist in binaries only and that men are rational while women are emotional. But, because the influence of hegemonic masculinity is so pervasive, even men in queer relationships—like ours—who resist hegemonic masculinity will feel bound to heteronormative gender attributes and roles, will experience the imperative of rationality. This is to say nothing of the fact that men in normative, heterosexual relationships experience this pressure too, regardless of the misogynistically farcical idea that is Freudian hysteria and female emotionality. Anxiety—by definition irrational—may complicate this masculine imperative, it may necessitate that partners decide whether they accept or reject this transgression of masculinity. It always was acceptance with you.

I had always longed to fall in love in autumn as upstate New York changed color. Like the maroon reds, flaming oranges, and amber yellows that crunch underfoot I wanted to float down, softly but inexorably, finally into your arms; and I did. It was the autumn of physics calculations, our charged exchanges of meterstick and stolen brushes of fingers on hands. It was the autumn of first dates, fire drills, an excuse to hold you close, of nights together...suddenly learning the topographies of skin, it was the autumn of butterflies and little birds, of doors barely a minute apart, our hearts closer, of safety in one another's arms, of what we called "felonious" kisses and "criminal" love.

It's late fall and we're lying in my bed. Ray LaMontagne's "Hold You in My Arms" plays: "It seems like everywhere you turn catastrophe reigns … I could hold you in my arms, I could hold you forever." An unwieldy map of Dickens' London — one I never reference — hangs next to the bed. Often it'll fall on us when we're tangled up in one another and often I cast it aside to the floor — without opening my eyes, taking myself out of the moment to think. I think you came to resent that I did, this heat-of-the-moment carelessness and disregard. It's around Thanksgiving vacation—late November or early December. I think it was late November, right before break (The first night back—early December or even later November—we were in your room. It was the first "Love you" that slipped out of my mouth. Was that the first time you felt you needed to say it back to me?). I'm holding you in my arms, your head resting on my chest; in this moment I am the embodiment of masculine firmness—solidity and stability…

"I told my little cousin E. about you," you murmur before continuing. My heart soars. "She said if you hurt me, she'll beat you up," you laugh.

"She'd be right to but I'm never going to hurt you."

"I know."

A year later, I'm behind deadline; OCD's completely stalled my progress. I tell you, "I'm spinning. I'm letting people down"; the masculine veneer of stability and rationality has begun to fall away. Despite your busy schedule you offer to get lunch with me and talk.

You reassure me that you're proud of me, that you love me…without once appealing to masculine norms of rationality, making me feel ashamed, without once chiding me for spiraling out of control.

You walk me back from lunch to my apartment in the rain.

Sensing my need to decompress, you ask me if I want to hang out that night. I say I need to write at first and I do. But after another four hours staring at the page and 400 words written—250's a great day for me—I convince myself that I deserve to decompress, I want to be with you.

So there we are in your room tangled up in one another (god how I miss your hands on my cheeks, your nails cutting through my hair). I've commandeered music privileges and turned on Ben Platt's "Ease My Mind." "When you collect me with your steady hand, with a language that I understand I feel put back together inside. You came out of nowhere and you cut through all the noise … Oh darling, only you can ease my mind," Ben sings. Today, it's been your steady hands holding me tight in my anxiety and that's alright for you, for me.

Around midnight I pull myself off the bed. You perch on the edge, dangling legs. I lean in to kiss you. I recall an ocarina-accompanied evening that first fall, your legs twined around my chest — how good that felt. "Can I hold you?" I ask. You nod. I wrap my arms around you and pick you up.

But it isn't like last fall. You tell me to put you down with panic in your voice. I do.

You tell me you don't like being held.

"I'm so sorry!" I blather, penitent but confused...

"It isn't your fault."

But suddenly the pent-up anxiety about deadlines and falling short and writing, the baseless fear of breaking my promise, of hurting you and that E. will abhor me (Does she still ask about me?) come crashing down. Everything begins to whirl, my frontal lobe bears down hot on my eyeballs, I begin to see flashes of color; I feel like I'm going to faint, or die.

"I'm overwhelmed right now and…I'm really not feeling well. I need to sit down." I do in your windowseat; it's the most readily available surface.

You could call me "hysterical" — invoke the normative limits of masculinity and popular notions of

Freudian emotionality. Instead, seeing I am drenched in sweat, you bring me a water bottle then sit down next to me. And when I need space you give it to me. When I don't, you hold me. You make me feel so safe.

You walk me back to my apartment in the dead of night.

"Please sideline work for the night," you urge me at the door. "I care about you. You matter so much. Whatever you need I am there." In this moment, it feels like we're a unit, an army of two.

In these moments, Prévert's *petites secondes d'éternité*, these untellable small and sweet moments of eternity, I feel so loved by you.

The first night back from summer vacation we are lying on our sides, with our heads at the foot of your bed, our eyes locked on one another. You ask me a question: "In five years are we…?" After "In five years are we…" though I don't comprehend much else; I know I want a future with you and that you might want one with me is everything I need to hear.

I ask, "Do you think about us together — five years from now?"

You shrug equivocating, "I don't know…"

I'd planned on waiting another four or five months to have this discussion but the question's out there suddenly and my anxiety and chronic uneasiness with uncertainty demand to know in order to be allayed—not all or any of the minutiae at once, just if you've considered the possibility.

I clamber to gain control of the lump in my throat but it's surged upward—washed over me; I choke out, "I am terrified of losing you."

You could say "Stop freaking out," positioning my emotionality as transgressive otherness, an unsightly spectacle even. But you don't; you snuggle in close and wrap your arms around me. "I'm not going anywhere," you promise, and I believe you.

I don't really get an answer but this is enough for tonight.

I do get a sense in the conversation, though, that your reticence might have something to do with a perception that I'm sacrificing for a future with you. When we met I wasn't yet skeptical of academia, was planning on going to graduate school for a doctorate; maybe you're worried I'm sacrificing that.

Maybe you're worried I'll ask you to compromise your aspirations for me. Maybe you're anxious about physical closeness. But as I have said, the joy of being with you encouraged me to reevaluate my priorities; I'm not sacrificing, wasn't sacrificing, I am advocating for the fulfillment I want in my life now.

Three weeks later, I explain all this to you, hoping to have more fruitful discourse about the future but you are even more unresponsive.

Four months later, in late January, the last time I try talking with you about it, we break up…

Before we do, though, we do talk about the future very briefly, how space and communication would work; I'm considering moving to Saratoga Springs to be with you through the remainder of your undergraduate career, figuring out what's next after we've both graduated. You don't love that idea but you do love your space and distance both physically and emotionally. "I'm getting better with distance and not overcommunicating," I say, "it's getting easier," as if wanting to be connected with you in some way is something to be excused; it's getting easier to just adapt, to compromise myself and my needs — to be someone I'm not, someone who doesn't accentuate or advocate for the intimacy and closeness he desires. When a person's tormented by his peers in early life it becomes easy to accept what he's given; I'd gotten used to feeling loved by you, and was scared of not having that anymore… I am sacrificing in this way to preserve the possibility of a future with you…

I need to tell you about something. Six months before we began dating, I found out my ex-partner (if we can be labeled "partners") had withheld information and misled me.

We fell for one another in a cappella my first semester but played dumb for almost a year; in late August—five months into COVID—we share our feelings by phone.

She's back at school, I'm remote and I say, "I don't expect you to wait for me."

"I'm not looking to see anyone until you're back," she promises.

Eight months later — finally vaccinated and preparing to come and see her — I find out she's been involved with other people for six months. When I ask her "Why?" she counters, "You weren't here": distance is to blame and it's my fault.

I didn't tell you when we began dating and had that conversation about past relationships; I didn't want you to think of us as a rebound — we weren't. After that I still didn't tell you because I convinced myself it's my own baggage to work through. The reality is that I didn't want to admit that I withheld something from you; I didn't want to hurt you. I still don't. I hope you can forgive me.

As a person who loves space and distance, given the opportunity, you become aloof sometimes. These periods of emotional and physical distance are understandably triggering for me; not hearing from you for a day or two, I reach out asking for reassurance that you and we are alright. I position my anxiety as arbitrary but it isn't. Indeed it wasn't always this way; in my relationship with K. we went several days to a couple weeks without talking. You're able to give me reassurance. But then the distance will return.

I wonder sometimes if things would be any different if I'd told you about K. — rationalized my anxiety to you. Would we still be together? Would you have been able to remain closer? I don't think so. I know you to be an amazing disability ally. Without reinforcing problematic imperatives of rationality (e.g. soliciting justification for my anxiety) you always reassured me when I was anxious... This isn't to say that talking through anxiety is suspect — just that care shouldn't be contingent on rationalization. And it never was with you; thank you for cripping heteronormative imperatives of rationality and teaching me that my anxious, irrational self is lovable. Even if things were different I don't think I'd want them for two reasons: you'd be uncomfortable with the closeness and rationalizing my anxiety to you would capitulate to societal imperatives of heteronormativity and masculinity. This also isn't to say that it was right of me to withhold it from you when it wasn't about rationality.

To crip heteronormative gender attributes, like rationality, is to crip hegemonic masculinity. Nearly a quarter of a century ago (in his 1999 "The Sexual Politics of Disabled Masculinity") disabled social scientist Tom Shakespeare called for the redefinition of masculinity "in … more open, more acceptable ways, which draw on the lived experience of men and the potentiality of men for change" (63). Hegemonic masculinity idealizes stoicism as courage and condemns emotionality as weakness. But counterdiscursive courage and strength could involve facing emotion. This I did with you often from breaking down about our future to the guard-down moments I miss. I also have done it—faced emotion—herein, in writing our story. Indeed this collection of essays that being with you inspired is my contribution to an interrogation and redefinition of hegemonic masculinity twenty-five years overdue.

One of us reluctant toward closeness, the other with abandonment trauma and anxiety, we just weren't capable of loving one another how we each needed. I need intimacy and you need space; this is difficult to reconcile. It hurts that I can't love you how you need because I do love you and that you can't love me either because we were something transcendent... But, if love is something you want for yourself in this life I hope you find the distance in it you need. I hope for myself that I find the connection I've been searching for. And I hope that we will stay in touch—no matter the time, the distance, the miles in between.

More than anything else I hope that we continue to allow ourselves to be complex, messy human beings. That we continue to take up space, be loud, and demand inclusion, that we advocate for ourselves and serve our brethren, that we help others to feel security and pride in their identities. That we speak truth to power, write against prejudice. And that we disrupt static normalcy with radical love.

Bolt, David. *The Metanarrative of Blindness: A Re-reading of Twentieth-Century Anglophone Writing*. The U of Michigan P, 2016.

Couser, G. Thomas. "Signifying Selves: Disability and Life Writing." *The Cambridge Companion to Literature and Disability*, edited by Clare Barker and Stuart Murray, Cambridge UP, 2018, pp. 199-211.

Crow, Liz. "Including All of Our Lives: Renewing the Social Model of Disability." *Encounters with Strangers: Feminism and Disability,* edited by Jenny Morris, The Women's Press Ltd, 1996, pp. 206-226.

Friel, Brian. *Molly Sweeney*. Penguin Books Ltd, 1994.

Gerschick, Tom. "Toward a Theory of Disability and Gender." *Signs: Journal of Women in Culture and Society*, vol. 25, no. 4, The U of Chicago P, Summer, 2000, pp. 1263-1268.

Love, Heather. "Stigma." *Keywords for Disability Studies*, edited by Rachel Adams et al., New York UP, 2015, pp. 173-176.

Mapumulo, Bongani et al. "Physical Disability and Masculinity: Hegemony and Exclusion." *Physical Disability and Sexuality: Stories from South Africa*, edited by Stine Hellum Braathen et al., Palgrave Macmillan, 2021, pp. 87-103.

Michalko, Rod. "'I've Got a Blind Prof': The Place of Blindness in the Academy." *The Teacher's Body: Embodiment, Authority, and Identity in the Academy*, edited by Diane P. Freedman and Martha Stoddard Holmes, State U of New York P, 2003, pp. 69-81.

Milton, John. "Paradise Lost." *The Complete Poetry and Essential Prose of John Milton*, edited by William Kerrigan et al., Modern Library ed., Random House, Inc., 2007, pp. 293-630.

− − −. "Samson Agonistes." *The Complete Poetry and Essential Prose of John Milton*, edited by William Kerrigan et al., Modern Library ed., Random House, Inc., 2007, pp. 707-761.

Ovid. *Metamorphoses*. Translated by David Raeburn, Penguin Books, 2004.

———. *The Metamorphoses Of Ovid.* Translated by Michael Simpson, U of Massachusetts P, 2001.

Pater, Walter. "Conclusion." *Literature and Culture at the Fin de Siècle,* edited by Talia Schaffer, Pearson, 2007, pp. 10-12.

Rée, Jonathan. *I See a Voice: Deafness, Language, and the Senses — A Philosophical History.* Metropolitan Books, 1999.

Shakespeare, Tom. "The Sexual Politics of Disabled Masculinity." *Sexuality and Disability,* vol. 17, no. 1, Springer, 1999, pp. 53-64.

ANXIETY PRESS